EDITED BY
PHILIP TALLENTIRE

CARLTON
BOOKS

First published by Carlton Books 2007

This book is not an officially licensed product of
Middlesbrough Football Club

Text and design copyright © Carlton Books Limited 2007

A CIP catalogue record for this book is available
from the British Library.

ISBN 978 1 84442 093 3

Printed in Singapore

INTRODUCTION

LIFE is seldom dull at the Boro. Promotion, relegation, promotion, near-misses, cup glory, cup heartache, you name it, Boro's loyal supporters have experienced an emotional rollercoaster in 130 action-packed years. And if the action on the pitch has been memorable, the club has also boasted its fair share of off-field fun and games down the decades.

There hasn't been much in the way of silverware to show for endless league and cup campaigns, but Boro's many great teams have left us with memories galore. Legends have come and gone, but will always be remembered. And a new generation of heroes are emerging on Teesside, ensuring a bright future for one of English football's most fascinating footballing hotbeds.

To read the inside story of Boro's never-ending quest for glory, simply turn the page!

❛I started going to Middlesbrough games with my father when I was a young boy. It was always my dream to play for the club... it's brilliant for me. It's the first time Middlesbrough have come for me, so I had to say, "yes".❜

Jonathan Woodgate *signs a loan deal with his hometown club in August 2006.*

With special thanks to Alastair Brownlee, Century FM, Middlesbrough FC and the *Middlesbrough Evening Gazette*.

The following resources proved invaluable in the compiling of this book: *Ayresome Park Memories* by Eric Paylor and John Wilson (Breedon Books); *Extra Time – The Official Biography* by Willie Maddren with Dave Allen (The Willie Maddren MND Fund 1998); *Golden Boy – A Biography of Wilf Mannion* by Nick Varley (Aurum Press); *Cloughie: Walking on Water – My Autobiography* by Brian Clough (Headline); *The Football Grounds of Britain* by Simon Inglis (Collins Willow); *Farewell but not Goodbye – My Autobiography* by Sir Bobby Robson (Hodder & Stoughton); *A Miller's Tale* by Alan Miller (Hessay Books); *Riverside Rollercoaster* by Graham Bell (Middlesbrough Football & Athletic Club 1986 Ltd); *Talking Middlesbrough – George to Juninho* by Paul Thompson (Legends Publishing).

'E-I-O, E-I-O, E-I-O, E-I-O, E-I-O, E-I-O,
E-I-O, E-I-O, E-I-O, E-I-O, E-I-O, E-I-O, E-I-O,
E-I-O, E-I-O, E-I-O, E-I-O, E-I-O, E-I-O, E-I-O,
E-I-O, E-I-O, E-I-O, E-I-O, E-I-O, E-I-O,
E-I-O, E-I-O, E-I-O... '

Boro fans' *unique terrace chant of celebration*

' Where will it all end? **,**

An MP's question in Parliament following Alf

Common's world record £1,000 transfer from

Sunderland to Middlesbrough in 1905

"Boro were the perfect scoring machine. No centre-forward in the game can take a ball through like Camsell."

*The **Evening Gazette** reports Boro's 10-3 thrashing of Sheffield United in November 1933. George Camsell scored four*

'We lost 1-0 at York City, who were in the Third Division North. It was my worst moment as a Boro player. With the team we had we should have won the cup that year. '

*Winger **Ralph Birkett** rues Boro's fifth round*
FA Cup defeat in February 1938

❝ There's absolutely no doubt that we would have gone on to win the championship but for the war. We had a great dressing room full of great characters. And we had great players like Bobby Baxter and Micky Fenton. I don't think anything would have stopped it. ❞

George Hardwick, *Middlesbrough full-back 1937–1950*

‘We had some good players, but it wasn't the same side after the war. ’

Wilf Mannion, *Boro legend 1936–1954*

‘I honestly believe that had it not been
for the war, Middlesbrough would have won
everything… they had so many great players. ’

George Hardwick

The biggest disappointment came the following season when Burnley beat us in the sixth round on a disputed goal.

Dickie Robinson *regrets Boro's FA Cup failure of 1947*

'We had a lot of laughs. The one thing which really sticks out was the day that Micky Fenton got a brand new Jaguar. He was really proud of it and we thought "We'll fix him". So the groundsman, Wilf Atkinson, and I got a pail of whitewash and painted it all over Micky's new car. Micky wasn't too pleased! ,

Rolando Ugolini, *Boro goalkeeper 1948–57*

> **❝** I could have gone anywhere, the clubs were coming here putting blank cheques in front of them trying to sign me. But the club just wouldn't let me go, the players had no power then. **❞**

Wilf Mannion

> **Play for Middlesbrough or no one.**

The **Middlesbrough board** *turn down yet another transfer request from Wilf Mannion, who responded by going on strike in 1948*

I worked at Cargo Fleet at the time and used to turn up for training in my work clothes. When I got back to the dressing room afterwards, I couldn't find my clothes. Micky had pinned them to the ceiling. And my boots were fixed to the wooden floor with nails hammered through the soles.

Alan Peacock *reveals Micky Fenton's mischievous side*

'Micky used to sit in the dug-out and, if the weather was terrible, and you got injured on the far touchline, instead of running over, he used to shout for you to come over to him for treatment. '

Alan Peacock *recalls Micky Fenton's coaching days*

‘I thought it was the end of the world.’

Ronnie Dicks *on Boro's relegation from*
Division One in 1954

❝Middlesbrough never bought the right players. They would buy men who were finished. There was no ambition.❞

Alan Peacock *explains why Boro failed to fulfil their potential in the late 1950s and early 1960s*

❝ We had a great forward line. We had three international forwards… but we never had the defence to match. When we scored at one end, the defence let one in at the other. ❞

Brian Clough, *Middlesbrough striker 1952–61*

'It was very frustrating. We were always up there, but fell away at the end of every season. I felt sorry for Stan (Anderson) because he did everything he could. He believed that the team could do better. '

Gordon Jones *rues missing out on promotion in the late 1960s and early 1970s*

‘ I'm not proud of some of my tackles, but it was a very physical game in those days and you couldn't just walk away from it. ’

Eric McMordie, *tough-tackling Boro midfielder 1964–75*

‘The largest and most significant football ground yet to be abandoned in the wake of the Hillsborough disaster.’

Simon Inglis, *stadium expert, writing about Ayresome Park in 1996*

‘Wilf Mannion was a hero of mine.
He was one of the greatest – one
of our national heroes.’

Sir Bobby Robson, *ex-England manager and lifelong*
Geordie fan reveals his admiration for a Boro legend

❝He played football the way Fred Astaire danced. He glided through every movement, every routine. He was a genius of his time.❞

Brian Clough *on his boyhood hero Wilf Mannion*

'Bob Baxter was one of the greatest players I ever played with as well as being a clown. He was a fantastic man.'

George Hardwick

> ❛Jimmy Gordon was called the hardman of Middlesbrough. He was only 5'8" or so but he would tackle anything.❜

Johnny Spuhler

‘I used to impersonate the manager Bob Dennison and one day he turned around and caught me. I think the writing was on the wall after that. ’

Rolando Ugolini *unwisely upsets the boss*

> ❝ That was a case of Wilf Mannion at his best. I've seen Wilf play some wonderful games but that was the best. ❞

Johnny Spuhler *recalls Boro's Mannion-inspired 5-1 win over Manchester United*

‘They had professors running the course. One of them told me that he wanted me to shoot at goal from a distance. The Portsmouth goalkeeper was in goal and I beat him and scored. The professor then came up to me and told me that I hadn't kicked the ball right. ,

Micky Fenton, *scorer of 162 Boro goals, had no time for the boffins at a Birmingham University coaching course*

'We had a great team before the war. Everybody said that we would have gone on to win the league if it wasn't for the war. But when we came back after the war, most of the side had broken up. Most of the players were too old. The team wasn't anywhere near as good. '

Micky Fenton

❝His attitude was that he was there to score goals, and he did. But when he wasn't scoring he wasn't interested.❞

Ronnie Dicks *evaluates Brian Clough's contribution*

'He was a great finisher and a very dedicated footballer. He deserved more caps, but then people couldn't always come to terms with his manner. He always let people know what he thought. '

Harold Shepherdson *on Brian Clough*

'After 354 first team games and 21 goals, my career was over and it hurt like hell.'

Willie Maddren *on retiring due to injury at the age of 26*

'Jones was a great player. He had the best left peg I have seen. He could have been a world class player. '

*Boro keeper **Willie Wigham** praises team-mate Gordon Jones*

“I still dream about that one against Manchester United, running down the left wing and hitting it perfectly. ”

John Hickton *re-lives the sizzling goal he scored against the Red Devils at Ayresome Park in the FA Cup sixth round, February 1970*

'There are some good players here, some mediocre players and some bad ones. '

John Craggs *recalls Jack Charlton's analysis of the Boro team he inherited in 1973*

'We ended up with a victory margin of 15 points and that was under two points for a win. It was certainly the best season of my career and a great achievement for the side. '

Jim Platt, *Middlesbrough goalkeeper 1970–83*

❝That first season was marvellous. There was a real party atmosphere towards the end of the season.❞

David Armstrong *remembers the 1973–74 promotion campaign*

‘Jack (Charlton) and I got on great, but we argued almost every day.’

Stuart Boam, *committed central defender and Boro captain 1971–79*

❝ At Birmingham we let them (the fans) down badly, it was heart-breaking. We'd beaten them twice in the league but just didn't perform. ❞

Frank Spraggon *rues Boro's FA Cup*
quarter-final defeat in1975

❛ If there was one season I look back on and wonder what might have been it was the 1974–75 campaign. Middlesbrough could, and perhaps even should, have been crowned champions of England. ❜

Willie Maddren, *Middlesbrough centre-back 1968–79*

'Jack Charlton's unwillingness to plunge into the transfer market for a striker almost certainly cost us the title.'

Willie Maddren *identifies what went wrong in 1974–75*

'It was very frustrating. We had a very good side and we could beat anybody on our day. The biggest problem was that Jack wouldn't spend the club's money. If we had bought a top quality striker in the mid-seventies we could have gone on to be anything. '

David Mills, *Middlesbrough striker 1968–79 and 1984–86*

❛ I should have spent the money we made at the club. **❜**

Jack Charlton *regrets penny pinching*
during his time at Boro

❝He could never remember our names.
He'd say "You there" or "Thingy".❞

David Armstrong *remembers*
Jack Charlton's hazy memory

❝Without a doubt, Jack was the man who sorted me out.❞

Graeme Souness, *battling Boro midfielder 1972–78*

❛In training, Jack would sometimes set the dogs on us! **❜**

Stan Cummins *recalls one of Jack Charlton's more bizarre training rituals*

❛ Alan would trip over the ball nine times out of ten, but if you knocked it in front of him and let him gallop after it, he was brilliant. ❜

John Craggs *on Boro's secret attacking weapon, Alan Foggon*

' Alan was affectionately known among the supporters as "The Flying Pig", such was the excess weight he was carrying. '

Willie Maddren *on Alan Foggon*

‘ Get the fat b**tard off. **’**

Willie Maddren *recalls a Chicken Run regular's not so*
affectionate demand for Foggon's substitution

❝ John Craggs should have got an England cap. When Steve Whitworth was selected ahead of him I thought it was an injustice because he wasn't in the same class as Craggsy. ❞

Peter Creamer, *Middlesbrough 1972–74*

‘My big favourite was Terry Cochrane. He was a brilliant winger in his day. And there was also Jim Platt in goal, he was one of the best keepers ever to play for the club.’

Former British boxing title winner **Cornelius Carr** *reveals his boyhood heroes*

'My only regret is that we never got to Wembley. We had our chances. We should have done better against Manchester City in the League Cup semi-finals and we should never have lost to Orient in the quarter-finals of the FA Cup. '

Jim Platt

❝ John Neal was a good manager. He wanted us to express ourselves and he was keen to bring the kids through. Craig Johnston, David Hodgson and Mark Proctor all came in and did well. ❞

David Armstrong *on the Neal era*

❝John was a mild-mannered man. He wasn't a raver. Sometimes, when he was talking, you couldn't see him for the smoke from his cigarette, but he knew his job and was very thorough.❞

Mark Proctor *on John Neal*

❝ 99 times out of a 100
I would have put that away,
it was one of those things. **❞**

Billy Ashcroft *rationalizes his infamous FA Cup*
quarter-final miss against Orient in 1978

‘Tony McAndrew would never settle for second best. He was always ready to put a boot up someone's arse.’

Billy Ashcroft, *Boro 1977–82*

> ❝ He called us Tweedle Dum and Tweedle Dee… we were inseparable. ❞

Dave Hodgson *reveals John Neal's pet name*
for him and Mark Proctor

'If I ever look back to a turning point in the history of Middlesbrough FC it has to be the FA Cup quarter-final defeat at Wolves. I have never felt so low, so hurt and I collapsed. '

Dave Hodgson, *Middlesbrough striker*
1978–82 and 1987

‘In my study I have two League Championship medals and two League Cup medals but I would have given it all up for the chance to be like Tony Mowbray. I envy the players who spend a decade at the club they love.’

Dave Hodgson

'It was the natural thing to do. Like them, I was a working class lad who was supporting his side. At the end of the day, every club is about the fans. They are the people that really count. '

Dave Hodgson *explains why he would watch Boro from the terraces when injured*

‘When I was 14 we were at Leeds and suddenly found ourselves surrounded – they knew we were Boro. We got the sh*t kicked out of us.’

Bob Mortimer *of Vic & Bob fame*

❝ It's an impossible job and, by the way,
I've recommended you for it! **❞**

Jack Charlton *stands down as caretaker in 1984 and*
hands the chalice to Willie Maddren

‏**❝** Middlesbrough were concerned about relegation from Division One and wanted me to help revive their team, not just as a sideshow to bring in a few quid. But I didn't join. The timing wasn't right… so I said "thanks but no thanks". **❞**

George Best *reflects on an invitation to join Boro in 1982*

'The whole Boro episode was a disaster before I went back, when I was there and when I left. I really wish I'd never done it and I bet Boro did too.'

Dave Hodgson *on his ill-fated return in 1986*

❝I was quite young when I was asked to get involved and then I was up to my neck in it. You never knew how bad the situation was. Every time you picked up a stone, something crawled out. I was told the debt was £1.3m – the turnover of the club was only about £200,000 – but that became £1.5m, £1.8m and £2m.❞

Steve Gibson *relives his mission to rescue bankrupt Boro in the summer of 1986*

‘ 100,000 tell me they were there. **’**

Steve Gibson *recalls resurrected Boro's first game,*
a 2-2 draw with Port Vale at Hartlepool in August
1986, watched by 3,456 loyalists

"Bruce was the perfect man for the job. He created a special feeling within the club. He was such a strong personality, but we needed somebody like that. He got the best out of everybody. "

Tony Mowbray, *Middlesbrough lynchpin 1981–91*

'If I had to fly to the moon I'd take Tony Mowbray, my captain, with me. He's a magnificent man.'

Bruce Rioch, *Boro manager 1986–90*

He used to give great talks and make you feel as though you were Real Madrid when you went out on the pitch.

Bernie Slaven *on Bruce Rioch*

     ❝I still say some of the football played between 1986 and 1988 was some of the finest anybody in Middlesbrough will have seen.**❞**

Gary Gill, *Middlesbrough midfielder 1983–90*

'Our team spirit was fantastic, I've never played anywhere where it's been better. The crack in the dressing room was the funniest you'll ever come across.'

Gary Gill *fondly recalls the post-liquidation days, 1986–1988*

' Some people think that a football dressing room may be stony ground for Christians but I think it's a brilliant place. '

Devout Christian and former Boro winger **Alan Comfort**

❝I thought that we would bounce back up again. We got a great start, but it didn't happen for us. The lads were older and didn't respond in the same way. I think Bruce had gone as far as he could go.❞

Bernie Slaven *admits Boro's bubble burst following relegation in May 1989*

' I didn't realize that the Boro team was so young. I think I was the only player with children. And everybody seemed to have blond hair, I thought I might have to dye my hair. '

Mark Proctor *rejoins bottle-blond Boro in 1989*

'We had a great side. Everybody worked for everybody else. But we were probably promoted too quickly. We weren't ready for the First Division and came straight back down. '

Bernie Slaven, *Boro striker 1985–90*

❝I just and kept on running. Then, when I cut inside in the Millwall half, their defence just opened up. I knew I was going to score. It was a wonder goal, the kind you dream about. ❞

John Hendrie *describes his incredible solo effort against Millwall in October 1990*

❝The most memorable occasion was at Wolves. When we had Nicky Mohan sent off and were a goal down, disaster stared us in the face but we rallied, scored twice, and earned our place in the Premier League.❞

Jimmy Phillips *recalls Boro's 2–1 win at Wolves in May 1992*

❝ I'm such a big Boro fan I find it strange to face them. The Blackburn players pick up on it. I get some stick from them because they know Boro are still my team. **❞**

Stuart Ripley *admitted he found it tough going home to Middlesbrough with Blackburn in 1995*

> It's always hard as a local lad, especially if you are a fan of the club. I used to get so cut up when results went against us. I used to feel murdered if we had been beaten on a Saturday.

Jamie Pollock

‘ I remember playing Bolton in front of less
than 7,000 people at Ayresome Park in 1993
so it was tremendous to turn out before nearly
30,000 Boro fans in our first game at the
Riverside two years later. ’

Jamie Pollock

There were car loads of people arriving at the same time, all just to stand and stare in awe. I did myself almost in a trance. I was reminded of the end of the film "Close Encounters of the Third Kind", where people were simply drawn to the spaceship.

Bob Mortimer *on the construction of the Riverside in 1995*

‘Nigel represented everything that a captain should be on and off the pitch. He gave everything for this club and was a real 110 per-center.’

Steve Vickers *praises skipper Nigel Pearson*

‘Nigel was the best captain that I have ever played with. He was such an influential player to have in your side – as important to Boro as a skipper as Roy Keane is to Manchester United.’

Derek Whyte *puts Nigel Pearson's contribution in perspective*

> **'** I was a bit disappointed when Barmby was sold because he was a very talented footballer who played for the team and could have provided me with a lot of good balls. **'**

Fabrizio Ravanelli *misses his assist machine, Nick Barmby*

❝Juninho jetted into Teesside today and the whole place has gone Samba mad. He looks tiny and reminds me of jockey Frankie Dettori.❞

Boro goalkeeper, **Alan Miller** *in October 1995*

‘Bryan Robson went all the way to Brazil to sign me and showed that he really wanted me at the club, that he really liked my football.’

Juninho *explains why he chose Boro*

'Today Wimbledon very difficult, long ball, long ball, us we pass, pass, pass, pass, pass, pass, pass, cross goal, 1-0, Yarm 85, lager, beer, Macky Millers. '

Alan Miller *recalls Branco's team-talk and post-match celebration plans, April 1996*

' Playing in an FA Cup final after leading the team out in the semi-final at Old Trafford. That season holds a lot of the best memories along with some of the worst – relegation at the end of it. ,

Robbie Mustoe *looks back to the 1996–97 campaign*

’I still can’t get my head around what happened that year because in the cup games we played really well, and also in our home league matches. But away from home we lost most of the games. I can’t really put my finger on what went wrong.’

Juninho *on the rollercoaster 1996–97 campaign*

' There was a fight and Coxy and Ravanelli were involved but to say everyone was rolling around in the grass outside the hotel is a bit over the top. **'**

Craig Hignett *sets the record straight about the punch-up between Fabrizio Ravanelli and Neil Cox on FA Cup final morning, May 1997*

‘Hey, who's that gadgie (bloke) with Wilfie (Mannion)?’

Boro fan *outside Wembley before the 1997 FA Cup final. The answer was Pele*

❝Emerson started like a house on fire for Middlesbrough. In his first seven or eight games he took the Premier League by storm. But once he knew Barcelona wanted him it poisoned his mind. **❞**

Boro chief-executive **Keith Lamb** *explains why Emerson failed to fulfil his early promise*

❝ People from the club tried to be friendly. They invited us to eat but it was all this heavy food. And I couldn't understand anything they were saying. ❞

*Emerson's wife **Andrea** explains how she failed to bridge the culture gap in England*

‘When we played at Derby that season I had a vest under my shirt that had "Where's Emmo?" written on it. If I'd scored I would have pulled it over my head and shown everyone. ’

Craig Hignett's *light-hearted response to Emerson going AWOL*

A Ferrari without a garage.

Italian journalist **Giovanni Galavotti** *describes Fabrizio Ravanelli training at Boro's less than glamorous facilities*

‘We used to play with smoke from the chimneys polluting the pitch. The pollution was so bad I didn't even send my son to school.’

Fabrizio Ravanelli, *Boro striker 1996–97*

> **❝** I never said such things. I only said the town was different from, say, London or Rome. I was happily settled and felt very good in Teesside as I was living in a beautiful village. **❞**

Fabrizio Ravanelli

> **❛**I was glad he went, his cup final display was daylight robbery – he only went on the field for a medal.**❜**

Ronnie Dicks *on Fabrizio Ravanelli*

❛I was actually one of the players who was sick at the time. There was a virus going around the club and something like ten of us had been on our sickbeds, so to say that we felt hard done by would be an understatement. ❜

Mikkel Beck's *verdict on the FA's decision to dock Boro three points for failing to fulfil a Premiership fixture at Blackburn in December 1996*

'We weren't treated fairly.'

Steve Gibson

‘We knew we had to get rid of players who were not prepared to fight for this club. ,

Steve Gibson's *reaction to relegation in 1997*

❛ Paul Merson was absolutely vital to us in our promotion campaign and signing him was a statement of intent. It showed everyone that we were not going to lay down and accept relegation. ❜

Keith Lamb, *looking back to the 1997–98 season*

I may have to quit for my health's sake. A lot of players at Boro like to drink and a lot like to bet. I know if I keep being exposed to drinking and gambling I am in danger of going back to my bad old days.

Paul Merson *in August 1998*

❝When he came out with those comments it was an insult to lads like Robbie Mustoe, Steve Vickers, Gianluca Festa and Mark Schwarzer and the foreign lads who are not heavy drinkers. We haven't got that sort of culture he was talking about.❞

Bryan Robson

‘We're actually quite a tame bunch. I don't think a Tuesday night out once every six weeks is excessive.’

Robbie Mustoe, *Middlesbrough midfielder 1990–2002*

' I was struggling to cope and I was a long way from home. The fact is it was nothing to do with Middlesbrough Football Club. I could have been at AC Milan, one of the world's biggest clubs, and I would still have left. '

Paul Merson *sets the record straight*

❝When he came to us he said he would not walk out on Middlesbrough like Emerson and Ravanelli, but he has done just that.❞

Keith Lamb, *1998*

❝I shouldn't have gone back. I didn't find a good atmosphere in my second spell here. I was on loan here the second time – it was not the same.**❞**

Juninho *regrets returning to Boro in 1999*

❝I had to make a change. It was no slight on my staff, we'd all been at Boro for seven years. But certain players had got too familiar with the set-up. I had to turn it round. Terry was the one man I could think of to do it. So I went for him.❞

Bryan Robson *explains why he asked Terry Venables to help him rescue Boro from the foot of the Premiership in December 2000*

' A lot of people, some of them close to me as well, have said that I sacrificed myself by doing what I did in bringing Terry on board. I didn't see it that way, I thought we needed a different voice around the place. I didn't want to let it stagnate, to stand back and do nothing, then still go down. **,**

Bryan Robson *denies accusations that he precipitated his own downfall by turning to Venables*

❝ I've left Boro in the Premiership, which was always what I wanted to do. Actually that's not quite true. I took them to three cup finals, where they'd never been before. But I had set my eyes on being the first manager in their history to deliver a major trophy. ❞

Bryan Robson *departs with honour in June 2001*

'Not so long ago, Boro were awful so I was always cracking jokes about them. But since they started doing well all my Boro gags have gone down the tube. Bryan Robson has a lot to answer for. '

Roy 'Chubby' Brown

❝ After relegation we did well to get out of the First Division at the first attempt. I hated football at that level… it wasn't football, it was all long ball. ❞

Gianluca Festa, *Boro fans' 'Player of the Season', 1998*

'It was the most wonderful experience to find myself playing alongside people of the calibre of Juninho, Ravanelli and Emerson. '

Robbie Mustoe

❝I have not spoken with anyone regarding a move away from Middlesbrough, nor do I want to. My family is settled on Teesside. We're all very happy… I want the fans to know I'm not looking at moving anywhere.❞

Christian Ziege, *June 2000*

‘For all my good feelings about Middlesbrough, I'd like to go to Liverpool.’

Christian Ziege *changes his mind, August 2000*

❝I came to the Riverside a few times as a Liverpool player and I could tell it was an absolutely fantastic place. The fans are so passionate and really get behind the team.❞

Paul Ince *signs for Boro in July 1999*

❝ I live within six miles of the ground and have done for ten years, so I know what an impact the football team has on the area. ❞

Kevin Keegan *witnesses Boro's rise*

‘ We felt we had gone as far as we could with Paul and that he had gone as far as he could with us. We felt it was in the best interests of both parties if we could arrange a mutual split. ,

Steve Gibson *on Paul Gascoigne's departure in July 2000*

'We sat down and talked and I felt I couldn't give him any more. I felt I had gone stale and needed a change, while I needed to give Bryan a breather!'

Paul Gascoigne, *Middlesbrough 1998–2000*

❝ I'm leaving behind a friend in Bryan Robson.
He did really well for me and so
did Middlesbrough. **❞**

Paul Gascoigne

'All the stuff about being a drinking club, or having players not good enough, I treat as rubbish. You can't let players do what they wish and be professional. That's a fact. As for the team, Boro had two internationals when I got there in 1995. Now they have more than 15 and they didn't cost the fortune some suggest. '

Bryan Robson *hits back at his knockers and defends his Boro record before handing over to Steve McClaren*

❝ I am very happy to be here. I think the club is capable now of doing better than ever before. I believe in Middlesbrough, it's like I am coming home. ❞

*Third time lucky for **Juninho**, who re-signed for Boro in July 2002*

❛We heard the news of George's death early in the morning. He's one of the greatest players ever to play for Boro and he'll be looking down and be very, very proud of the boys.❜

David Parnaby, *Academy Director, dedicates Boro's 2003–04 FA Youth Cup win over Aston Villa to legend George Hardwick*

‘ I'm very proud – the boys have been fantastic over the two legs against a very accomplished Villa side. We did a very professional job and ran out worthy winners. I felt quite emotional after seeing the lads doing a lap of honour and carrying the cup around. To see the fruition from the programme is wonderful. ’

Youth team coach **Mark Proctor's** *joy at Boro's FA Youth Cup final win*

‘The bottom line is that we need to produce players. It's wonderful that we've won the tournament for the first time, but we do realise that our ultimate job is to put people in the first-team environment for the manager to hopefully pick.’

Mark Proctor's *words proved to be prophetic*

❛ Zenden's penalty, it should have been an indirect free-kick to us. I don't want it to sound like sour grapes but it was a major incident in the game. ❜

*Bolton boss **Sam Allardyce** was far from happy with Boro's second goal in the Carling Cup final, February 2004*

‘ Coming here for a third time and getting another opportunity... I feel this title is as important as the World Cup. ’

Juninho *celebrates the Carling Cup final win over Bolton*

❝I refused. It was nothing against Celtic, I just did not feel I could be thrown out like that. I had a great relationship with the fans, I felt I would be betraying them. I even offered to stay and fight for my place.❞

Juninho *rejects Celtic, August 2004*

'McClaren just looked at me and told me he did not want me any more. He said he was going to change the whole team and I did not fit into his plans. I was part of the past. '

Juninho *explains why he signed for Celtic just days after turning them down*

❝ He used to sh*te, but now he's all right.
Bolo, Bolo Zenden. ❞

Boro fans *express their new-found*
appreciation of the mercurial Dutchman

'Get in yer big Aussie. Mark Schwarzer is the greatest Australian hero since Ned Kelly.'

*Century FM commentator **Alastair Browlee** hails Boro's keeper following the penalty stop from Robbie Fowler which cemented UEFA Cup qualification, May 2005*

"I was staring at Middlesbrough keeper Mark Schwarzer from 12 yards, knowing that I had one kick to put us into Europe. He saved it. The f*cker saved it."

Robbie Fowler *from* **Fowler: My Autobiography**

‘Boro had no fight, no nothing. When I saw the fourth goal go in it was too easy for Villa. It did break my heart seeing it. The emotions took over and I just went. It triggered something. I started running through the stadium and saw a gap and just went. I was cut up with anger. I was angry with McClaren for his decisions and selections. It was instinctive to throw my ticket at him. ’

Mark Davison *explains why he marched from the North Stand to the dug-out to register his disgust at Boro's 4-0 defeat to Aston Villa, February 2006*

'I fully understand the frustrations of everybody and the anger, because we have let the fans down at home. They have every right to say what they want to say and to criticise and to demonstrate. We have to make sure we do something about it. I take responsibility for that and only we can get out of it and that's what we are going to do. '

Steve McClaren

'I'm losing football matches and it's my job to win them. Of course I'm feeling the pressure but I'm the manager, I take responsibility and I'm not going to panic, but hold my nerve. We need the senior players to be strong and show their experience and their leadership. There are no excuses. '

Steve McClaren

‘Steve wasn't under pressure from me.
I remember saying to him after the Villa game
that we have to take this on the chin, go home,
think about it and come up with solutions. ,

Steve Gibson

‘We got ourselves into positions where things were getting a bit hairy at times.’

Mark Schwarzer *on Boro's 2005–06 mid-season wobble*

'It was a proud day for Middlesbrough Football Club and a proud day for our chairman Steve Gibson. It has been his dream to field a team of players who were born within 30 miles of the stadium. Out of the 16 players in the squad, 15 were born within that radius. You will be hard pressed in history to find a team as young as that, all English and with most of them born within 30 miles of the club. '

Steve McClaren *picks a starting XI at Fulham in May 2006 that included ten homegrown players with four more on the bench*

'If I go home and find Massimo Maccarone in bed with my wife, I'm going to ask him if he wants another blanket. '

Boro fan's *reaction to the Italian's miraculous late winner which gave Boro a 4-3 aggregate UEFA Cup semi-final victory over Steaua Bucharest in April 2006*

❝ Goooaaal Maaaassiiiimo Maaccaaaroneee… Maccarone's header and Boro have stuck a stake to the heart of Dracula's boys. ❞

*Century FM commentator **Alastair Brownlee's** reaction to Boro's remarkable comeback against Steaua Bucharest*

'It's Eindhoven, Boro have made it, one of the most glorious nights in the history of football. It's party, party, party, everybody round my house for a parmo – we're there!'

Alastair Brownlee *greets the final whistle in the UEFA Cup semi-final, second-leg*

> It's absolutely brilliant that we've reached the final of a European competition – it's like a dream come true for me.

Stewart Downing

❝ Sometimes it goes in,
sometimes it doesn't. **❞**

Mark Viduka's *philosophical response to being*
denied a crucial equalizer by Sevilla keeper
Palop in the 2006 UEFA Cup final

'We have a very disappointed squad of players. But this was never a four-goal defeat and the players shouldn't be down. We have proved already in this competition that we can play. It's just a pity we fell at the final hurdle. It was one game too far for the squad after 64 games.'

Steve McClaren's *UEFA Cup final verdict*

> Sevilla started better than us but we knew at half-time that we could play better and that's what we set out to do. In the second half we created two great chances and their keeper made a great save from Viduka. In addition to that, we had a stonewall penalty turned down and that could have turned the game.

Steve McClaren

'To reach the final is a phenomenal achievement for a small town in Europe.'

Steve McClaren

‘We have enjoyed some marvellous occasions and Boro will always remain close to my heart. I'm so pleased I was able to deliver success to Middlesbrough because everyone – especially the fans – deserves it. ’

Steve McClaren's *parting words before taking the England job*

"You have to look at what he has left behind. Two FA Cup semi-finals, two (cup) finals, one of which we won. It's now up to someone to take that forward."

Gareth Southgate *highlighting Steve McClaren's achievements, not realising he would end up in the Boro hotseat*

'They can't do it, it's as simple as that.'

John Barnwell, *Chief-Executive of the League Managers' Association, responds to Steve Gibson's plans to appoint Gareth Southgate*

‘ It's no secret that we spoke to Terry Venables and Martin O'Neill, and then I look at our club and what we need. If I make a list of the values I'm looking for in a manager, a certificate does not even come on to the radar. ,

Steve Gibson *explains why he turned to the unqualified Gareth Southgate*

‘I think I have somebody here in Gareth with all the experience, with good judgment and who possesses the character, the intellect, the determination to turn his experience into the criteria we are looking for. He is one of the most intelligent and potentially great managers of his generation. ’

Steve Gibson

'One of the reasons I got this job is because the chairman knows how committed I am to the club. I have been here for five years and I have a great affinity to Middlesbrough. '

Gareth Southgate

❝I want to attack. I want to play an attacking brand of football next season. That's not to say we want to win games 8-6 every week. But I am mindful of how expensive it is for supporters to watch Premiership football these days. Fans pay a hell of a lot of money to come and watch us and we have to do what we can to send them home with a smile on their faces. ❞

Gareth Southgate

‟I played my way into the side when I had a good training session the day before the derby match. I kicked a few of the lads and the manager saw that. „

Lee Cattermole, *17, explains how he earned his debut at Newcastle in January 2006*

> ❝The very thought of walking into Ayresome Park at that time was like a Catholic walking into the Vatican.❞

Middlesbrough-born **Harold Shepherdson**
on signing for his hometown club in 1937